THE UTHER SAGA

Uther - Part 2 - Dragon Publishing 2025

Paperback ISBN 978-1-063794-2-0

Illustrated by Thannis ©

Text by IamKDK ©

UTHER

Part 2

Written by IamKDK

Illustrated by Thannis

Contents

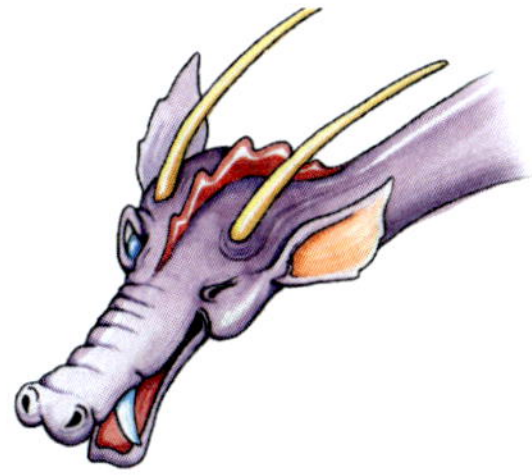

Meet the Characters 6

Your Quest 8

Introduction 9

Chapter One - The Shadows 11

Chapter Two - The raffle 24

Chapter Three - The Child Catcher 37

Chapter Four - The Train 51

Chapter Five - The Volcano 63

Chapter Six - Uther's Training 73

Chapter Seven - Egor the Indigo Dragon 87

Chapter Eight - Dragons Unite 95

Epilogue 109

Acknowledgements 113

About Me 115

Meet the Characters

THE DRAGONS

Uther

Ragna

Pilot

Ashan

Egor

Silo

OTHER CHARACTERS

Witch Fanella

Randalph
the Raven

Xavier
the Octopus

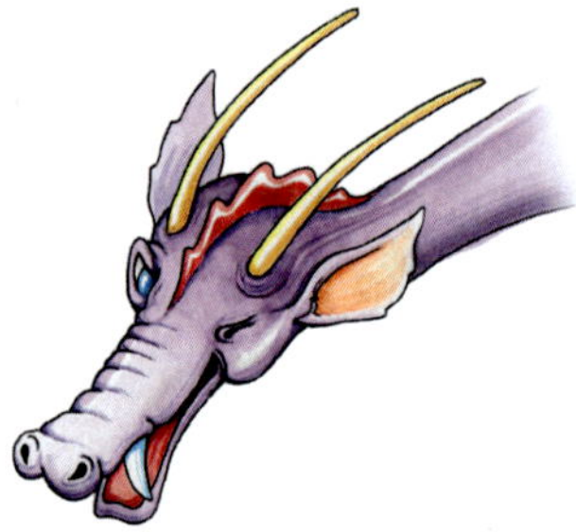

Your Quest

Uther has set you a challenge again. At the end of each chapter, you will see a short rhyme with a picture guiding you to find an object. Uther had so much fun hiding these items and hopes you enjoy this extra quest. At the end of the book, if you have found all the items, you will be awarded a Gold Star, the ultimate award from Uther!

Uther wishes you luck in completing this mission.

Introduction

Uther Part 2 has more of Uther's adventures, as he continues to help humans and dragons unite on this beautiful planet.

He has ups and downs along the way, Egor makes sure of that, by trying to interfere and upset his plans on many occasions, but Uther never gives up on his quest.

In this book, Uther has gained new helpers; Ragna, Pilot and Ashan, who are young green dragons that Uther has known since they hatched.

They are keen to learn to support and help Uther on his mission, also devoting their time to helping humans and dragons understand and help each other.

It's not an easy task, and Uther is nurturing these youngsters to be an asset, as the world needs the Dragon Army on call for the future.

Come and join us as we travel with Uther and his friends to new places, meeting more people and new dragons along the way. The emails will keep arriving.

Chapter One

THE SHADOWS

Pirates are found on every coastline
Hiding in caves, carefully leaving no sign
They plunder ships and lands for their wealth
Keeping it for themselves, known for their stealth.

Their ships are large with massive sails
Always carrying different flags to hide their trails
The crew were often desperate men
Hiding past lives of badness over and again.

One crew in particular were very rich
Keeping all their treasure in an obscure pitch
A dry cave situated beside the sea
People guessed, but no one knew where it could be.

Everything seemed safe for the Blackjack pirates
Then they made a mistake stealing from The Tyrants
They were thieves, who stole from the King
The army looked but couldn't find the King's ring.

Uther was desperate to help the King
It was evil to steal the sovereign's ring
If no action were taken, they might steal the crown
A King with no crown might look like a clown.

The King was respected across all the lands
This latest disrespect affected all he commands
His soldiers were worried, how this had happened
It actually made the garrison saddened.

That day came, Uther blew flames in despair
The palace attacked, the King's army not there
The crown of the King, was taken by force
The Tyrants laughed without any remorse.

Would The Tyrants or Blackjack steal the crown?
As a symbol of control over every town
The people were afraid, was their King weak
Would it be families next that the pirates would seek?

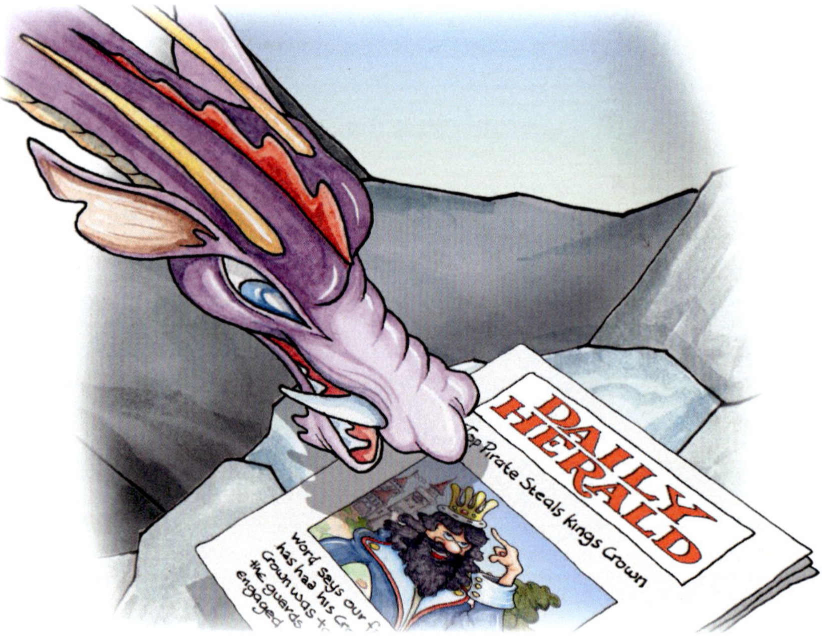

Uther got mail, as if it were needed
The Daily Herald reported, its return was pleaded
Blackjack responded the very next day
A page with Blackjack wearing the crown in play!

The black, toothy grin sent the town into shivers
Across the highest hills down to the lowest rivers
There was talk of defeat; the King was done
Uther knew differently; the day could be won.

These braggards were misinformed again
To raid the castle, they must be insane
You were really stealing from the people
They knew their actions were completely illegal.

Uther knew the secret of ancient days
He planned his move to grab their gaze
He located the base of Blackjack's lair
From high in the sky, he saw his black hair.

To lure out these pirates would take lots of skill
Involve them in thinking there was gold for the kill
If the Tyrants were trapped, the others would fail
Uther's plan was perfection in every detail.

Uther took a crate of gold from Blackjack's enclave
And placed it on the beach near The Tyrants cave
Blackjack wouldn't take long to come searching
The chest contained the gold crown he had been nursing.

Greed would be their downfall, he thought
He was certain that they could be caught
Viewing the beach, timing had to be precise
Uther had the best view that he'd checked twice.

Uther perched on the cliffs, watching with care
These rival pirates were blindly unaware
When the battle began then Uther would fly
Knowing what would happen if one of them should die!

Blackjack shouted at The Tyrant's guides
Return my trunk where the crown resides
You stole it yourself to make the King look weak
Why take it from me? Our association looks bleak.

The Tyrant appeared with a look of surprise
It was on our beach that trunk of disguise
You didn't return it? I thought that was quite strange
Their confusion gave Uther time to make the change.

Uther tested his skills as he flipped and spun
He almost lost his focus while having such fun
The Tyrant and Blackjack waved their fists at him
He didn't stop; he started to skim.

He came to stop on the beach with the pirates
Ignoring the abuse of those causing riots
He rested a claw firmly on the chest
This is going back to the King; I do not jest.

They screamed as they both blamed each other
Pistols were drawn, bullets looking to smother
Uther moved the crate out of harm's way
Watching and making sure there was no delay.

Blackjack fired first at The Tyrants chest
He fell to the ground, but no body lay at rest
Only a shadow was seen walking along the shores
As the rest turned to shadows, they'd settled all scores.

The shadows walked the lands forever and ever
The pirates' punishment, the return of never
It started as a fable from ancient times
Uther knew it to be true; he'd seen the signs.

These lost shadows would wander behind the good
A penance of time, as wickedness should
Uther knew this would happen if conflict occurred
The pirate's tale had again been stirred.

Uther was sad that this had happened
But pirates will be pirates, whenever maddened
Never considering that badness is always repaid
Uther watched their shadows, looking betrayed.

That's it, Thomas, get those teeth cleaned
Uther did it again; he's a courageous fiend
I bet the King was happy to get his crown back
Uther was jubilant in this attack.

I can't believe how amazing Uther is
He always deals with problems like an easy quiz
It's his intention to make badness pay the price
With a plan of attack, not the throw of a dice.

One more, please, Papa, Thomas pleaded
It's school tomorrow, your bedtime's exceeded
Climb into bed knowing Uther soars at play
Go to sleep and dream of Uther's amazing day.

IMPRESSIVE UTHER PREVAILS AGAIN -

The search quest begins...

Uther says the King's Ring was lost
Will someone find it? His fingers are crossed.

Chapter Two

THE RAFFLE

The fair arrived with everything to be tried
Win a goldfish and the dodgems to ride
The coconut shy, with coconuts to fall
The spirited music, a calling for all.

Win a fish with a hoop, or maybe some candy
Fire the rifle to win a teddy so dandy
The helter-skelter ride on a coconut mat
Or the ghost train, your own fear to combat.

Merriment fills the town with laughter
Once a year, the excitement before and after
Everyone comes together as they have much fun
It's been an annual event since it begun.

Understanding the town and its tradition
Only possible because of the mayor's decision
The crops were good, and the people had been busy
The whole town's anticipation left them in a tizzy.

Uther usually stayed far away
Too many people putting on a display
This year would be a new kind of joy
There was a raffle, an enjoyable decoy.

The posters sat on the billboards so high
A raffle with a surprise, a secret in the sky
It was the major topic of the town
Everyone guessing, not wearing a frown.

The raffle tickets were selling well
Apparently, two winners would be swell
One boy and one girl would be the winners
Anticipation causing much talk over dinners.

In Uther's cave, there was chatter, too
Flame blowing by the youngsters, practices a few
The art must be practiced to accuracy gain
The youngsters grew fast, some with horns or a mane.

Sometimes there were BBQs, the odd little feast
Had to be discreet, with no music at least
If alcohol were consumed, it could be a disaster
No burning of local crops from a drunken blaster.

There had been incidents in the past
Dragons drunk and disorderly, flaming's were vast
Uther remembers a time from his dragonhood
No one forgot when a year's crops were lost for good.

Summers were different for dragons than winter
Many grazing animals, the land of the sprinter
They salivated a lot, that's dribbling like a stream
They kept away from the fields, no flaming extreme.

The day before the surprise raffle was drawn
The organisers were unsure what would be done
The surprise would be huge for everyone
But there was evil loitering to spoil this one.

The Indigo dragon sat watching the scene
That darn Uther, the helpful, likeable machine
Always saving the day, making dragons look soft
He wasn't about to sit back, whatever the cost.

Being friends with witches was always good
Especially for something to taint some food
He'd put a delicious treat near Uther's cave
He smiled inwardly, excited to have Uther his slave.

A fanfare was played, and the raffle was ready
Uther hid close by, feeling rather unsteady
He wasn't used to having the public so close
He hadn't factored Egor's jealousy to diagnose.

Before the raffle, Uther went to clean his fangs
Shocked to find his tribe sleeping on their hands
He saw the food that lay half-eaten
Gave it a sniff and knew how they'd been beaten.

There must be danger lurking for the raffle
I expect it's that Egor ready to snaffle
The children that win getting the scariest ride
Probably dropping them high and wide.

As he returned, he heard names being called
Eliza and Ethan, the winners looking enthralled
Awaiting their prize, which was the Uther sky ride
Egor perched to attack, ready to steal their pride.

No time to dither, although Uther had to consider
How to divert Indigo with a massive skidder
He dove from the tower above the town hall
Through the clouds, exhaling a momentous squall.

Indigo was shocked and scared to see Uther
No avoiding the attack, it couldn't have gone smoother
Uther had grabbed a big sack from the front of his cave
Which he placed over Egor, it was a close shave.

He pulled the rope, swinging Egor over his left shoulder
Everyone gasped seeing Uther retrieve him like a boulder
Flying high into the sky, heading over the moon
His brothers waiting with the great chains of Boon.

They were ancient chains that restricted flight
They were cursed by old witches, no dragon's delight
Indigo screeched as they popped on the chains
Flew him to Toad Island, croaking filled his brains.

Uther gathered himself and practiced his smile
He had children awaiting their prize for a while
Gently, he landed to huge gasps and a few shouts
Proudly, he announced Egor's whereabouts.

Eliza and Ethan had seen Uther afar before
Heard of his heroic stories, also his loud snore
They didn't know their ticket was to fly and soar
Both were so excited they fell to the floor.

Uther rallied them around and helped them alight
His big eyes peered into their faces of delight
He bowed to the crowd, waved his wings in respect
Pushing off from the grass, smoother than they'd expect.

Everyone saw as they soared through the gears
The children's heads tucked behind Uther's ears
Squeals of delight, as he flew gently to land
Knowing he'd saved the day, hearing the sound of the band.

The King gave a wave; he could rely on this dragon
The band played Three Wheels on My Wagon
The villagers happily danced the evening through
Uther snored, whilst dreaming of Egor eating toad stew.

IMPRESSIVE UTHER PREVAILS AGAIN -

The search quest continues...

Everyone needed a ticket to enter the raffle
Maybe you can find one, or will it you baffle?

Chapter Three

THE CHILD CATCHER

Children often play happily in the street
Laughing and playing, oblivious to who they'll meet
Sadly, children go missing daily as they play
No one knows why they suffer this way.

It's been a problem in different reigns
Sometimes it ends with the culprits in chains
The parents are vigilant on most days outside
But children are sneaky, and sometimes they hide.

Jingling bells are heard at 4 pm daily
Children are taken as they play gaily
It's thought they are taken on the King's orders
Being delivered as a payment across the borders.

That's only the story told by sad parents
Children enticed by sugar fancies so pleasant
Most children are taught to avoid all sweets
Believing that keeps them safe on the streets.

Older children fear for their younger friends
The child catcher wasn't about to change his trends
They heard the children were in the woods
Having to chop trees and work for local hoods.

Uther was a concerned dragon from what he'd heard
How was everyone being so blurred
He waited for an email recently dated
He waited, he waited, and still he waited.

Stories were becoming more desperate to hear
These children must live in utter fear
Why would this happen to ones so young
The wicked witches' orders came from her tongue.

Take all the children who eat sweets
The ones who refuse can stay on their streets
I'll show that town how fickle their children are
I'll take them to teach them a lesson afar.

It had begun as a trick on the town
Wicked witch Fanella would bring them down
The children accepted all the sweets in droves
They were put to work to pay for their clothes.

Uther was mad, Uther was angry
That wicked Fanella behaved so badly
So, before the help email arrived, Uther was gone
He flew scouring different woods 'til dawn.

The woods and forests were all so dense
He had to take care to avoid every fence
The sharp branches catching wings would easily tear
His only concern was how the children were, and where?

He finally found many children huddled
Hungry, tired, and cold, very muddled
They were constantly guarded by angry men
Who watched and shouted again and again.

A plan was needed to guide the scared kids
He had to be measured in making their bids
For freedom to be back with their petrified folks
Gentle persuasion, nothing that provokes.

There was a consideration in these desperate times
You needed to be ruthless, not just give fines
Aggression could work now, needing many a suture
A fight would be felt, but what of the future?

Uther thought he could just flame the witch
Leave her sizzling in a ditch
But that wasn't Uther's usual style
He started his plan without being hostile.

The wicked guards were only there out of fear
They didn't want any spells from witchy dear
So, he laid a trail of gold coins to the woods
Now to get their attention for the precious goods.

Uther watched as each guard took their shift
There was one called Marty, who deserved a gift
He was kind to his captors, gave them extra food
Discreet but kind, he must be good.

The trail of gold caught everyone's attention
They started to leave by stealth without a mention
Only Marty remained, so Uther landed close
The children stared in awe; Marty comforted most.

Uther fired the woods, showing Marty the path
To lead the poor children away from the witches' wrath
Marty understood Uther's kindness in his heart
His bright eyes were clear right from the start.

Uther gave a toothy grin and a kindly wink
The children knew he'd save them; Marty needn't rethink
The thought of the spells Witch Fanella could cast
Made Uther decide to end things with a blast.

Fanella was busy in her filthy den by the ocean
Squashing beetles and dead toads for her next potion
She saw flames roaring on the distant hilltop
No idea of Uther's ideas to make her drop.

She got on her broomstick, leaving potions brewing
Uther knew she'd respond, leaving wickedness stewing
As she flew to the hills, Uther appeared in the skies
Throwing flames into her home, ashes her surprise.

She turned on Uther, bemused, and amazed
How dare this pitiful dragon leave her fazed
She took chase, no time for creative spells
She would track him down wherever he dwells.

Uther knew surprise was his best chance
Her broomstick was no match for his dance
Hiding in a small cave next to the sea
He knew she had seen him, so she knew where he'd be.

She didn't stop to think; she charged into the cave
Uther relied on this, for this fight, he'd be brave
She entered the space; Uther barged her passed
Grabbing her leg in his jaws, she was aghast!

He flew her right above the clouds
Shouting his spell loudly for all crowds
Ditch this Witch, this Evil Witch
Make her suffer and live in a ditch.

In a complete daze, Fanella repeated every word
Stuck in a trance, from all that she'd heard
She would stay in this trance for the next thirty days
Uther's wry smile, one eyebrow to raise.

Uther left Fanella babbling her utter rubbish
Toad Island made everyone feel rather sluggish
Uther thought this was fitting after all she had done
Flying over the town, he watched the children run.

He soared proudly over the King's castle
Another drama, he'd managed to unravel
He saw the parents hugging their tired children
The streets would be safe now he'd dealt with the villain.

I love Uther, Jemima said to her dad
What's the next story? Will Uther be mad?
That's enough for now, Jemima, only one story per night
Get some sleep with Uther, on your sleepy flight.

IMPRESSIVE UTHER PREVAILS AGAIN -

The search quest continues...

Witch Felena lost one potion as she fell
Maybe it's hidden somewhere under her spell?

Chapter Four

THE TRAIN

If Uther ever saw youngsters in the sky
He would often join them to watch how they fly
If they were a bit ragged, he'd stay a bit longer
They needed to know how to get stronger.

A cold winter's day, Uther surveyed the lands
Ice settled on his wing tips, little icicle bands
The air was crisp, a nice air to inhale
Lying over the lands like an icy veil.

Flying like this as the skies were clear
Seeing for miles, he saw young dragons appear
He knew these three since they were hatched
Ashan, Pilot, and Ragna, three lads well matched.

These green dragons were great at flying fast
Beating their hatchlings, most they surpassed
Uther flew up beneath them, making them jump
They became unstable, Uther's mischievous bump.

Keeping them steady, making the boys gently drift
The four looked magnificent, smooth, and swift
Looping the loop in unison, so much fun
They were glad that Uther had joined in this run.

Uther knew that these youngsters were now drakes
No longer sitting in caves flaming shapes
They were getting stronger and always aware of the land
The time would come when they could lend a hand.

The railway tracks below looked shiny
The coldness freezes any trace of oil, slimy
A distant train sounded weird on its tracks
Its grip was uncertain, like slipping on wax.

Ragna heard it too, and gave Uther a look
Uther sensed his notion, like reading a book
The four landed on the highest point
Pilot was the watch out who would not disappoint.

Watching, they chuntered about flying in the cold
As the train approached the tunnel, so old
Chugging to the entrance, with the wheels slipping
It was obvious to see that nothing was gripping.

Six golden eyes and two piercing blue ones
Watched the carnage hearing loud banging like guns
Slipping off the rails at pace and sliding onto its side
Blocking the tunnel, hearing screams as everyone cried.

Uther wasn't about to wait for an email
He directed his helpers to land in the dale
Scared and excited, they stood by Uther's side
Ready to help and save people, rescues implied.

Speaking to the yearlings he explained what to do
No heroics, assist safely, no time for review
People screamed as fire brigade alarms were heard
Uther's email must be buzzing, that seems absurd.

As the fire brigade arrived, Uther was waiting
He offered help, as the Chief was collating
Uther suggested the dragons could secure ladders in place
Allowing the firefighters to enter through the safe space.

The Chief was so happy that Uther was there
The young green ones concerned him, eyes so clear
Uther told Ashan to lift all the ladders into place
Whilst he guided Pilot and Ragna to secure them at pace.

People were shouting, the train had been packed
Ladders secured, so their help had an impact
Ambulances were slow to get to the scene
Uther organised the boys to offer a screen.

Uther understood the importance of speed
The injured being helped promptly was the need
Uther knew how his service could help more
Fly people to the hospital, straight to the door.

Platform pallets were made to fit each dragon
A human helping service, how could they imagine
They were ensconced in the world of Uther
Landing on the helipad smoothly was tougher.

They did so well to take the injured with care
The paramedics worked swiftly, the journey to prepare
It was a long tiring night; Uther had to admit
These young dragons knew how to commit.

The hospitals were wary as the first dragon landed
Nurses stayed inside; doctors demanded
Ashan flew first, and it was a nervous flight
Keeping steady and smooth, not causing a fright.

Pilot was next, three hurt children so small
He purred as he flew, was the children's recall
These dragons now understood Uther's purpose of living
For dragons to be seen differently, saviours, so giving.

The tunnel was blocked by the wreckage of the train
All passengers rescued, their help not in vain
The four dragons decided to give the firemen help
Pulling carriages out, straining with a screeching yelp.

The tunnel cleared, their day was a success
They were well organised, like a good game of chess
Ragna asked Uther; when could they help him each day
He said study hard, then in the future I dare say.

Despite being shattered, they dove into the lake
A welcome clean whilst diving, followed by a shake
Blew flames to the stars, as darkness descended
The flight home full of chatter of a day that was splendid.

IMPRESSIVE UTHER PREVAILS AGAIN -

The search quest continues...

A wheel from the train is missing
Uther requests your help before he goes fishing!

Chapter Five

THE VOLCANO

The caves were abuzz after the train incident
The Dragon Times full of praise for the vigilant
Ragna told Uther, that now, he was famous too
Uther smiled and winked, so proud of his crew.

He was impressed with the Drakes so young
Strong hearts, their praise should be sung
New dragon leaders in waiting, they were needed
Their protection and wisdom would be heeded.

Ragna, Pilot, and Ashan had a constant yearning
Uther stressed he required them to be learning
Show that dragons and people can share this land
But not everyone thought his plans were grand.

Other caves held only anger at Uther's tactics
Thinking his actions were misplace antics
What was the point of making dragons look weak
Humans should fear them, think their outlook is bleak.

It surprised Uther, the voices so different
How could the other greens be so ignorant
He moved the clock to see his mail
The news, earthquakes made the land frail.

The lands had been trembling in places faraway
Uther was always alert to his emails each day
He couldn't imagine how the planet would cope
If no one helped or offered any hope.

At three in the morning, the message came
The large volcano on Dvorak was no longer tame
The villagers below were scared for their lives
Uther took his area map from his archives.

This volcano could do major damage
Wipe out generations, how would they manage
Maybe if he flew there and actually saw
He could use his skills to create a safe corridor.

He rested no more; he had to leave now
He left a note for the elders, they'd know anyhow
The eruption was imminent, but it didn't say when
Uther took to the skies, flying over the glen.

He took a slight rest on his way
The journey was long, a tiring day
The horror he saw when he arrived
His worst fears were revived.

His plan could help; he had to start work
No time to waste, but no going berserk
If he could divert the molten lava when it blew
He could save the villagers from being fondue.

He looked at his map, he needed to flame trees
Pull up the roots, create a lava squeeze
As he was flaming the trees, he saw Ragna appear
The boys had followed without showing fear.

He explained his plan, and they framed the route
The volcano was bubbling, ready to shoot
The villages were empty, the people safely away
Diverting this chamber could solve the problem today.

The liquid spilled over and slid down the hill
No time to stop flaming the pathway, all using skill
What happened next was like a miracle
The old mines below the path started to fill.

Chapter Five – The Volcano

The path led the steaming liquid into the holes
Like ladling hot soup into endless bowls
Even the dragons were hot and needed to move
Ashan was warned as he hopped over each groove.

Pilot flew high to ensure nothing was missed
They couldn't let the rogue eruption cause a twist
All looked in order, it was filling the mines
With Molten lava in the old mining confines.

Today, they had halted the travelling heat
The national office could decide how to retreat
The land was so hot, the lava was underground
Everyone was safe, including every single hound.

The flight home took a long time
Uther flew gently with his new partners, no crime
Conserving what strength was left in the tank
The crusaders in motion, watching Uther's flank.

Heroes of the hour, the newspaper said
Dragons assisting humans, Uther slowly read
Uther's dedicated mission, required much change
His future visions journey covered a mighty range.

IMPRESSIVE UTHER PREVAILS AGAIN -

The search quest continues...

The lava was hot and washes stuff away
Where did Uther's map end up that day?

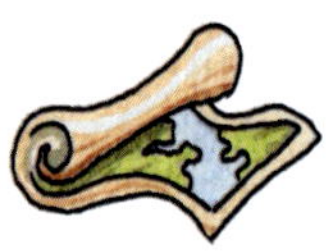

Chapter Six

UTHER'S TRAINING

Uther's responsibilities stretched rather wide
As hatchlings developed, they needed a guide
Uther had been busy away from the caves
Ragna reported to Uther about some daily raves.

Not all young had horns yet, but all were green
Pilot knew these gangly youngsters made a scene
Uther decided after speaking with the elders
To train these juveniles to be super welders.

All of the youngsters had heard of Uther
They heard of his conquests on the computer
To have him as your teacher would be an honour
Known in Dragon World, as the best dive bomber.

Uther decided that he'd set out a rota
To find out who was good in the water
All the dragons were green with gold eyes
Most were in for a shocking surprise.

Ragna, Pilot and Ashan, all had experience
Even an elder helped too, old timer Sirius
The young rebels had to show respect and learn
If called to help now, it would be a concern.

Training and examples of how to get better
Ashan and Ragna knew that they would get wetter
Most had eyes that glistened like gold
Uther hoped that underwater, they would be bold.

The draglings expected to just throw a few flames
Set woods on fire, play pyromania games
Swimming wasn't something most could do
The roll call announced they stood for review.

First, they were told to fly to the lake
As a team in motion, not making a mistake
No touching wings, but keeping in the shadows
Forget about flaming, stay aware, and composed.

Some were bemused. No flaming allowed.
A fluent trip high, then dive to the ground!
They were all calm as they perched around the lake
A few looked worried, perhaps they'd make a mistake.

The instructions were clear to each dragling
The training was working, all were poised to spring
Then the final words sank into their brains
Learn to dive, then swim, wanting no wing sprains.

They had never entered the lake before
Only skimmed it with feet, swooping to shore
Their gold eyes shone with fear more than glee
Uther calmed them down, as their honoured trustee.

Dragons have perished doing this in a rush
So, be calm and listen, wait in a hush
He had their attention, dragons going swimming
Paddling first, that had them grinning.

Dipping heads, bubbles blown through the nose
No flames or heat, just like air through a hose
They all mastered that in a quick time
They all trusted Uther, their fighter of crime

Young Silo thought he could just float on his back
That wouldn't help him much if under attack
Uther tried to display the danger of this
Shoving him sideways, his wings to dismiss.

He spluttered and choked a few wet flames
That should stop him from playing silly games
Logs were placed for a water landing perch
Flying down from the high steeple above the church.

It was all going quite well on the first day
Before going home, a water game to play
Suck in water, heat it with flames in the throat
Then throw it into the castle's big moat.

Get some good rest, as tomorrow gets tougher
Nothing too scary, he'd be their buffer
The objective this week was to help them dive
One day, they'd help humans to survive.

The cave was quiet that night, all tired, no rave
Many exhausted draglings after being so brave
Tired youngster snores, rang through the trees
Uther glanced over them, seeing some grazed knees.

Elders were grateful to Uther for helping this way
Uther knew discipline would be useful each day
There may be a time when all dragons unite
Stopping a major catastrophe in the dead of night.

Uther sat and heard sounds float in the trees
He heard Egor's moaning ride on the breeze
He was still on Frog Island under the spell
His lifetime punishment, forever to dwell.

Day two was busy. Excitement for the dragons
Strength building to start, pulling logs in wagons
Puffing and mild flaming, their muscles expanding
Uther watched as Pilot demonstrated log standing.

Day three; back to the water, gentle log landing
Most slipped splashing about, it was so demanding
They slipped and slid, some falling head-first
Losing their claw grip, like they were cursed.

Balance was explained by standing on one leg
No rolling about, like a precious little egg
They were becoming accustomed to getting wet
Diving on their minds, to be mastered as yet.

Day four: accuracy, flame small branches up high
Ashan said no burning whole trees on a fly by
Embracing discipline, the youngsters soaked it up
Ashan frowned at the odd wayward pup.

Day six, was the day when they learned to unite
Given a problem to solve, a few got it right
It's working as a team, not a race or even a game
Pull a large car from the lake, be strong, not lame.

Day Seven arrived, Uther watched them eagerly
In only a few days and they were balancing regally
Thinking of each other and how uniting worked
It astounded him that none of them shirked.

Strong golden eyes watched Uther intently
No one thought diving was just elementary
The secret, Uther said, is committing to good speed
Too fast, lacks control, or too slow can't succeed.

The earlier floater, sat with eyes like a psycho
The first picked by Uther was a reformed Silo
Always joking, but his expression was different
Each little dragon was calm, not belligerent.

Instructions explicit; horseshoe to be retrieved
Noisy, nervous clucking as words gently received
Silo showed great patience in controlling his speed
Breaking the surface, snout holes closed tightly indeed.
He kept his eyes open, not a moment wasted

Surprisingly like flying in water, as Uther had stated
Uther proudly observed from beneath the water
Silo exited with a horseshoe, to howls of laughter.

Not all were streamlined, but all were successful
They worked so hard, in the water so stressful
Routine practice was prepared for the pups
Forbidden forever, was flaming poor ducks.

Uther knew this would help him in the future
His emails came constantly to his computer
A team was needed to operate under pressure
The world was changing; it needed help in great measure.

News travelled fast through the Dragon world
Young dragon pups training, flaming curtailed
Uther created a lesson for all young to follow
Emails of success came from caves in The Hollow.

Uther was happy as he rested in his cave
Teaching those pups to be controlled and brave
It was the beginning of the main Dragon Army
Uther's long dream, now, not seeming so barmy.

IMPRESSIVE UTHER PREVAILS AGAIN -

The search quest continues...

Uther hid two horseshoes, but only one was found
Can you find the other one,
maybe dropped on the ground?

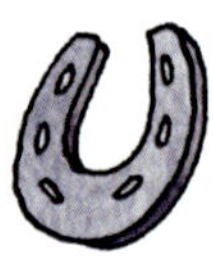

Chapter Seven

EGOR THE INDIGO DRAGON

Egor the Indigo dragon was green when hatched
There were two in his egg that perfectly matched
Egor was strong from whence he emerged
Kicking the twin dragon out, making him submerged.

Before he was one month old, he had turned blue
A sign to the elders to watch when he flew
He was always fighting and causing a scene
It seemed the only way he knew, was to be mean.

Uther had hatched at a similar twilight
He was a vastly different dragon, avoiding limelight
This annoyed Egor, he expected Uther to fight
Uther studied and always beat Egor, remaining polite.

It seemed Egor came first at being bad
It was good enough for him, he'd get Uther mad
Not Uther's intention: he came first at being good
Never changing the direction, he understood.

Every effort was made to temper Egor's mood
Not interested in changing and never subdued
It was only a small matter of time
Until he committed some evil crime.

He was banished from cave to cave
He was never going to be anyone's slave
Eventually, he flew alone in the skies
Searching to cause danger, no great surprise.

It was Uther's decision to cast the spell
To banish him to Toad Island to dwell
He was lucky in a complicated way
Who knew, it may be reversed one day.

Toad Island was noisy with toads loudly croaking
Nothing stopped them, not even occasional poking
The only place Egor could find some peace
A small, soundproofed cottage near to the geese.

The geese were noisy as well
They always chatted, lots to tell
The cottage was small but was his safe haven
The only visitor was an occasional jet-black raven.

Initially, Egor raged and raged
He felt the impatience of being caged
Recently since finding his small cottage of peace
A calmness of acceptance, there was to be no release.

The spell had made him a complete wreck at first
Heavy chains and he had an amazing thirst
He didn't know how long he'd even been here
Was it a month or even a year.

Days came and went; he did puzzles and read
He even taught himself to bake bread
If he thought about how he could fly or get away
The spell just became stronger, no way to stray.

He thought of Uther, the kind dragon so stupid
What sort of dragon liked playing Cupid
Helping rotten humans, who deserved to suffer
Why did humans like this pathetic flame bluffer.

He had never had contact with human beings
They are good as a light lunch were his teachings
He would never ever see Uther again
That's a relief, even if he was insane!

Randolph the raven came with fruit every day
Dragons hate fruit, but what could he say
Bring me a cow or a deer for my lunch
He only brought fruit for Egor to munch.

The toads were oblivious to Egor now
He was part of the landscape, like a moaning cow
That contributed nothing, but ate all the fruit
Next, that blue dragon would play the flute.

Egor sat doing sudoku when it happened
An email arrived, a note that threatened
Be ready at the cottage, I will be there at ten
So weird, who's coming? An army of men?

Was he to be given a deeper spell
He couldn't envisage living in the toad's well
He didn't want any change, he coped every day
Who was coming to see him? What would they say?

It was a definite order, not a request
Egor's mind was racing, who sent this bequest?
The letter was typed, not even a clue
Uther's note had him flummoxed and, in a stew...

IMPRESSIVE UTHER PREVAILS AGAIN -

The search quest continues...

Where did Randolph the Raven fly to hide?
They've been hunting far and wide.

Chapter Eight

DRAGONS UNITE

The world is changing at an amazing rate
Wetter, windier, hotter than any previous date
Disasters threatening the planet's existence
Uther's concerned; it needs so much assistance.

Uther knew something big could happen
He had a sense that could only come from a dragon
What if it were so large, he wouldn't cope alone
He prepared an email, he sighed, then groaned.

Dear Dragons of the World, I ask a huge favour
If we have a huge disaster, will we be the saviour
We should be a great army to save this world
Should something major happen and the planet be twirled?

Letters to help came back thick and fast
Even the strongest of them aware the calm couldn't last
In theory, the agreement was on the table
Who would be in charge, Chief being the label?

Uther's email had worried Egor to his gut
Who would visit him and for what?
When he sat in his cottage as ten was struck
Uther landed on the porch, hoping for luck.

The air was frosty between the dragons of fire
Egor saw Uther land, the dragon to least admire
What do you want? Wasn't the spell enough?
He fired at Uther, grey smoke with each puff!

The world situation was one for concern
He had a proposition for Egor to return
The dragon army intended for them all to unite
If there were a crisis, they would all need to fight.

But not fight with each other
No baby dragons to smother
But to unite with humans, our planet to save
Maybe lift Egor's spell, but he'd have to behave.

Egor stared in amazement into Uther's eyes
Green eyes of Egor, no thoughts could disguise
He'd have to think about this collusion
Helping humans, for him was a total illusion.

As Uther left, Egor knew this was his chance
He would help for a while, lead them in a dance
Uther would believe he was a dragon so weak
In the shadows of time, he would be free to speak.

Uther knew his game; but he had to ask
All the world dragons would help with this task
Strong Egor was a great swimmer, he could easily cope
As part of a great army, maybe a glimmer of hope.

The Dragon News was reporting on planet events
The latest, an avalanche, humans couldn't prevent
The banks of all rivers were close to flooding
Uther knew it was time; the Dragon Army was coming.

The email went out; the dragons were all on alert
Fast time was passing, their position to assert
When the flooding joined the avalanche
The dragon army offered its solid branch.

People were perishing as the banks were squeezed
By mud and water and the mayhem of this siege
The alarm was sent, the world's dragons appeared
Landing on local mountains, a place they had cleared.

Uther, Aragnos, Zeus, and Odin
Joined together to plan all options for choosing
Each leader would have a specific task
No confusion, no questions to have to ask.

Aragnos would deal with all the sliding mud
That would help to stop the shedding of more blood
Zeus and Odin would stem the water
Helped by Aragnos with a damn as they halter.

Uther's crew would move the people
They had this experience of major retrieval
The work began, busy dragons filled the sky
Lumps of iron bridge are dragged as they fly.

Uther had an idea of involving the sea
He dove into the ocean at a pointed degree
It was a hive of activity in the ocean below
The tremors were unsettling; all eyes were aglow.

He was greeted by many angry fins
Who thought he was coming to eat their skins
One creature knew better, and halted their fears
Xavier the octopus, he'd known Uther for years.

All the sea creatures gathered around
Uther went up for air or he would have drowned
Xavier organised all the sharks and the fish
Rolling rocks and debris, sea-breaking their wish.

Uther was amazed at how this emergency had shown
When uniting the planet, no one is alone
The Xavier army was building dams
Uther flew to ferry people who were scared like lambs.

The avalanche was slowing
The mudslides stopped growing
The water flowed less, everything looked calmer
Even Egor was helping to lessen the disaster.

After two days the leaders set a timetable
The work had to continue whilst they were able
The hospitals were full of people severely injured
Some dragons too, now their work was being hindered.

The work continued; humans looked timid
Although the firefighters were always rigid
Collaborating with dragons on intricate stuff
Smaller hands, unlike dragons, large and rough.

Four weeks went by, and the land settled again
All working together dragons and men
The sea creatures too, it was an amazing feat
They had all shown, there's no need to compete.

Some dragons initially, were constantly dribbling
Watching the humans, wanting to go nibbling
Their attentions were focussed, their work was to fly
Eating any humans would make tensions too high.

Xavier had done a brilliant job
All the seas united, a purposeful mob
The skies are full of dragons, not blue but green
A colour of the skies, never before seen.

The countries looked battered and bruised
Small shoots of vegetation looking confused
The rivers were flowing, and the fish were calm
The sea damns gently ebbed like a soothing balm.

All was repairing, and Egor was back
He approached Uther with a huge sack
These humans are stupid, they think we are slaves
We're in control; he shouts as his claws he waves.

Uther shook his head in despair
A harsh atmosphere, old times didn't compare
Egor demanded payment for all his efforts
Uther offered a spell, Egor fled for the deserts.

The land was safe again, people were mending
Thankful world leaders were messages sending
No one could remember how this all started
We do; it was Uther, our dragon, kind-hearted.

IMPRESSIVE UTHER PREVAILS AGAIN -

The search quest concludes!

The Dragon Newspaper gives the most news of the land
No one can find Xavier, maybe he got lost in the sand!

THE UTHER SAGA

EPILOGUE

When Uther shares his tales, I write
His expression is serious when describing a fight
He has laughter in his eyes most of the time
He dedicates his life to a balance, sublime.

He doesn't lose his temper if things don't go well
He says Well, it happened, so don't scream and yell
Dig deep and decide how to move forward
It may be a challenge, and not what you ordered.

He is not always right, but he's a positive dude
He treats everyone fairly, an admirable attitude
He longs for world peace and a world for us all
Animals, Humans, fat, thin, short, or tall.

I tend to agree with him about being kind
Understanding another's view, not being blind
To take a step back if it's aggrieved that you feel
Take a moment to finding kindness to reveal.

The problem is receiving words of aggression
Evokes a response of revenge, making them deafen
Be calm and cool, respond truly to you
Think why they have anger, understand their view.

Uther says it's not easy, but it does become so
Get your words from kindness, not the depths below
Fairness to others on our planet so blue
From the Oceans to the mountains, consider them too.

He mentioned the ocean and a few of his friends
The stories I'm writing, about how he defends
The planet and all its beautiful living creatures
A side Uther reveals, with all of its features.

Please join him next time as he dives into Uther 3
Finding fun, laughter, and some mystery
Sharing each moment that he has endured
To ensure that our freedom is always assured.

DID YOU COMPLETE THE QUEST?

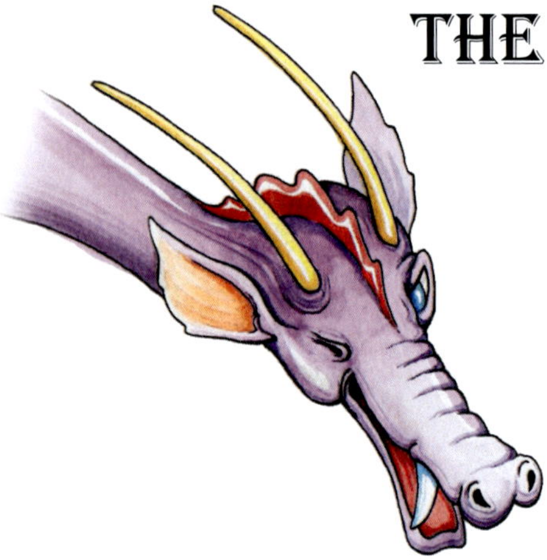

Uther hopes that you helped
him find things in each story
You've earned this Gold Star
to join the team's glory!

Uther is Good, Uther is kind
He'll be back soon; he's your dragon assigned.

Acknowledgements

Uther continues to lighten each day that I spend entranced by his charm. He is a delight to write about. I have some special people to thank for helping me tirelessly.

John, my ever thoughtful and patient partner, who

never admits he tires of hearing each verse as I write them. Then he sits and reads them too. Your support and belief are incredible. Thank you, my person.

Terry, my amazing illustrator, continues to amaze me with his talent, with endless illustrations of Uther on his travels. Uther is My Seat at The Table, both of which you have helped me complete, and given artwork that brightens each page. Thank you, Terry.

Maarten, my friend and web designer, has been highly creative in giving me the best website to represent me personally and has been meticulous in every detail of all areas. Thank you.

Lesley, my fabulous friend, and proofreader extraordinaire, who points out everything that I misspell or miss out, in a kindly fashion, without judgment. Thank you.

Last but not least, is Alexa, my publisher so special, who has been there with support and advice since Uther Part 1 needed her delicate touch and vision. Thank you for your belief.

I am hoping all the love and support continues through the rest of Uther's Saga. There's much more to come.

To all my friends and family who are supporting and believing in me on my journey.

A massive thank you xx

IamKDK

About Me

I am a very active person, who enjoys walking, cycling, and being outdoors. A walk in the park watching the wildlife whilst listening to birds singing away is a delightful way to spend a morning and prepares my day for writing Uther's stories.

I also enjoy going to the theatre, opera, restaurants, dancing, swimming, meeting with friends and family over a good dinner and a glass of wine.

My little office is where I sit and write mostly. I can focus without interruptions but can still hear the birds singing their songs, as they go about their daily business. When travelling, I often prepare a chapter or two on my phone or tablet, without the need of a pen or paper.

Uther is the centre of my writing world, and I never tire of his adventures. I have drafted books that are yet to be published following Uther and his friends through different worlds and scenarios, and the words are still flowing.

Uther is a culmination of my life's experiences and emotions, and he is literally My Seat At The Table, which is my adult poetry book about daily stuff, which everyone can recognise and enjoy.

I thank you for reading or listening to my book, as my stories continue to unfold Uther's journey through his life.

Until the next time we meet on Uther's pages and Uther prevails again.